Science Experiments

LEVERS, WHEELS, AND PULLEYS

by
John Farndon

BENCHMARK BOOKS

MARSHALL CAVENDISH
NEW YORK

Marshall Cavendish Corporation

99 White Plains Road

Tarrytown, New York 10591

© Marshall Cavendish Corporation, 2002

Created by Brown Partworks Ltd

Library of Congress Cataloging-in-Publication Data

Farndon, John.

    Levers, wheels, and pulleys / by John Farndon.

                  p. cm. - (Science experiments)

Includes index.

ISBN 0-7614-1341-3

    1. Levers-Juvenile literature. 2. Wheels-Juvenile literature. 3. Pulleys-
      Juvenile literature. [1. Levers-Experiments. 2. Wheels-Experiments.
      3. Pulleys-Experiments. 4. Experiments.] I. Title.

TJ147.F37 2001

621.8'11-dc21   2001035107

Printed in Hong Kong

PHOTOGRAPHIC CREDITS

t – top; b – bottom; c – center; l – left; r – right

Corbis: P5 Alison Wright; P6–7 Annie Griffiths Belt; P10–11 Paul A
Souders; P11t Bettmann; P14–15 Ric Ergenbright; P15t London Aerial
Photo Library; P 26–27 Duomo; P 28–29 Jean-Yves Ruszniewski
Galaxy: P5 Robin Scagell; P17 Richard Bizley; P20–21 Nigel Evans
Image Bank: P18–19 Terje Rakke
Leslie Garland Picture Library: P16; P23t
Pictor International: P4; P8; P19t; P22–23

Step-by-step photography throughout: Martin Norris

Front cover: Martin Norris

Contents

WHAT ARE MACHINES?

Even the most complicated machines usually incorporate one of five basic machines. Wheels and axles, for example, are a key component of every automobile.

Did you know?

The first known wheeled vehicles were wheeled sleds, as shown in ancient Sumerian pictures (from Uruk in modern Iraq) that date back to 3200 BC. And a pottery cup in the shape of a wheeled wagon was found in a grave in Szigetszentmarton in Hungary. This dates back to 2900 BC.

Wheels, levers, and pulleys are all machines—devices that make tasks easier for us to do. Some machines, such as screwdrivers, are simple. Others, such as washing machines and trucks, are much more complicated.

In the last 200 years, we have come to rely on a huge range of machines. Industries use giant presses, drills, boring machines, and lathes. Offices use computers, typewriters, and many other machines. Cars, buses, airplanes, and trains carry people around, while homes are full of machines from scissors to vacuum cleaners.

Some machines make it easier to move things—a door handle makes it easier to pull back the catch. Some machines move things that could not be moved in any other way, such as a dock crane that lifts a ship. When machines that move things are driven by natural energy such as wind, water, and coal, they are called "prime movers."

Some machines do not move things but instead turn one kind of energy into another. Refrigerators, for instance, use electrical energy to draw out heat and keep things cool.

There are five basic machines: the lever, the wheel and axle, the pulley, the wedge, and the screw. These simple machines can be used by themselves but

are often combined to perform more complex tasks. Even the most elaborate machines usually incorporate at least one of them. A washing machine, for instance, will typically have a wheel and axle to turn the drum, a pulley to link the motor to the wheel, screws to hold it together, and levers to open the door—and even a wedge for the door catch.

LEVERS

A lever is a simple machine that makes it easier to move a load by amplifying, or making bigger, the effect of the effort used. When you use a spoon to pry the lid off a can or squeeze the handbrake on a bicycle, you are using levers.

Levers were the first machines, and have been used since prehistoric times. When Stone Age hunters strapped a bone handle onto their stone axes to make their blows more effective, they were making a lever. When early farmers used long sticks to lift stones from the ground or turn over the soil, they were also using levers.

The simplest levers are nothing more than long, rigid objects, such as steel rods or planks of wood. One point on the lever, however, must be

A wheelbarrow makes it easy to move heavy loads because it combines a lever with a wheel and axle. The effort is provided by the muscles lifting the handles, and the fulcrum is the wheel on the ground.

Did you know?

Levers are used throughout the natural world. In fact, the human body has its own levers. Virtually every moving bone in the skeleton uses the lever principle. Your forearm, for instance, is a lever, with the fulcrum at the elbow. The effort is the forearm muscles; the load is your forearm, plus whatever you are holding in your hand. In the case of your forearm, the effort lies between the load and fulcrum.

In focus

LOAD AND EFFORT

The effectiveness of a lever can be worked out by very simple sums. The farther the effort is from the fulcrum relative to the load, the more effective it is. In fact, the load you can move with a certain amount of effort varies in exact proportion to its distance along the lever from the fulcrum relative to the load. If the effort is three times as far from the fulcrum as the load, it is three times as effective—and so you need a third of the effort to move the load. If the effort is only twice as far from the fulcrum, it is only twice as effective.

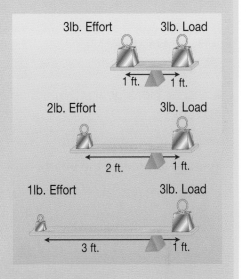

The effectiveness of a lever depends on the relative positions of effort, load, and fulcrum.

fixed to act as a pivot. Scientists call this fixed pivot point the fulcrum. If the lever is a plank resting on a log, the log is the fulcrum. When you lever open the top of a can using a spoon handle, the rim of the can acts as the fulcrum.

When a force such as human muscle power is applied to one end of the lever, it moves a load placed somewhere else along the lever. Scientists call this force the effort.

Just how much effort it takes to move a load depends not only on the size of the load, but where on the lever it is applied. When the effort is a long way from the fulcrum, or the load is

relatively close to the fulcrum, the effect of the effort is amplified—and so less effort is needed to move the load. When the effort is closer to the fulcrum, its effect is reduced and more effort is needed to move the load.

Because a lever is fixed at the fulcrum, the effort effectively turns the load in a circle. This is why the movement of a lever is called a turning effect (see page 22). Whenever you swing open a door, you make use of a turning effect—the hinge of the door acts as the fulcrum. The amount of force created by a turning effect is sometimes called the moment.

CLASSES OF LEVERS

You will need

- ✓ A plank of wood to act as a lever
- ✓ A shorter block of wood to act as a fulcrum
- ✓ Weights to provide a load
- ✓ Yourself to provide the effort

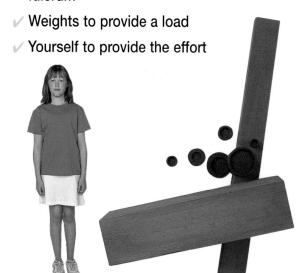

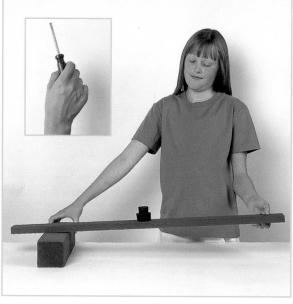

1 Rest the lever on the fulcrum, place the weights in the middle and lift the lever at the far end. This makes a Class 2 lever.

In the real world

SCREWS

Screws are one of the five basic machines (see page 5). They work by wrapping a groove around a shaft, in a very long spiral. This long groove means that the load—and so the work needed to push the screw in—is spread over a long distance. Screw threads are said to combine a lever—the screwdriver or spanner used to wind them in—with an "inclined plane." An inclined plane is a slope, like the sloping grooves on a screw, and is another simple machine; you need less effort to raise a load up an inclined plane than up a step.

Screws and bolts are ancient machines said to have been invented by Greek thinker Archytas in 400 BC.

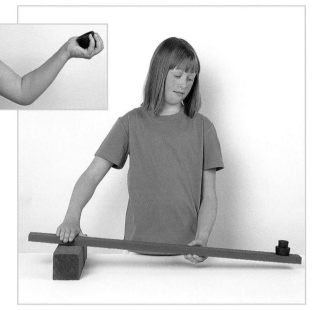

What is happening?

By swapping the places of the fulcrum, load, and effort on the lever, you are making three different Classes of lever. Class 1 levers, like scissors, have the fulcrum between the effort and the load. They are very effective but move the load in the opposite direction to the effort. Class 2 levers, like screwdrivers, have the load between the fulcrum and effort. Class 3 levers, like the forearm, have the effort between the fulcrum and the load.

2 Hold one end of the lever on the fulcrum, place the weights at the far end and lift it in the middle. This makes a Class 3 lever.

Rest the middle of the lever on the fulcrum, and place the weights on one end. Now try lifting the lever at the far end. You will find that the lever simply rises off the fulcrum and the weights don't move. If, however, you push down on the lever rather than lifting it, you will raise the weights easily, although you must take care to keep them balanced. This is a Class 1 lever. Now try lifting various weights with the three Classes of lever. Is one Class more effective than the others?

WORK AND EFFORT

In every machine, there are two main forces involved: load and effort. The load is the force to be overcome—that is, the force that is resisting movement. If a lever is lifting a stone, the load is the weight of the stone. The effort is the force used to move the load.

Machines work by cutting the effort needed to move a certain load. The amount a machine cuts effort is its mechanical advantage, or MA. To calculate the MA, scientists simply divide the load by the effort. When a machine gives MA it does not add energy. The total energy needed to move the load is always the same, with or without the machine. A machine works by spreading the force needed. A machine typically moves a heavy load a short way by using a weak effort moving a long way. A 10-lb. load might be moved 1 ft. by a 1-lb. effort moving 10 ft. The distance moved by the effort divided by the distance moved by the load is called the velocity ratio, or VR.

The work done by the boy in lifting the sack depends on how much force he uses to lift the sack, and how far he lifts it.

In focus

UNITS OF WORK

Scientists measure work in units of force and distance. In the United States, the unit is the foot-pound—the work done when a force of 1 pound moves an object 1 foot. In the metric system, the unit of work is the joule. This is the work done when a force of 1 newton moves something 1 meter. So a joule equals 1 newton-meter.

ARCHIMEDES'S MATH

The Ancient Greek scientist Archimedes was not the first to realize that machines make tasks easier, nor even the first to work out that a small effort can move a large load, if it is spread out over a long distance. But he was the first to prove it—and prove it mathematically. He also showed that work, effort, load and everything else can be predicted mathematically. This was the first time that math was used to understand the physical world, but it proved so successful that math is now the basis not just of all machine engineering but all advanced science.

An imaginary portrait of the Greek scientist Archimedes.

In theory, the MA and VR should match. If a load is 10 times the effort, for instance, the effort must move 10 times as far. But no machine is perfect, since friction and other factors impair efficiency. So effort goes to waste and does not move the load as far as it should. In a machine that is only 50 percent efficient, a 1-lb. effort moving 10 ft. moves a 10-lb. load only 0.5 ft.— not 1 ft. as it should if it was 100 percent efficient. In fact, most complex machines are much less than 50 percent efficient.

Ultimately, what counts in a machine is how far the load moves, and the effort it costs to move it. Scientists call this the work done. Work is the force applied multiplied by the distance moved by the load.

WEIGHTLIFTING

You will need

✓ Three friends of nearly equal weight

✓ A seesaw

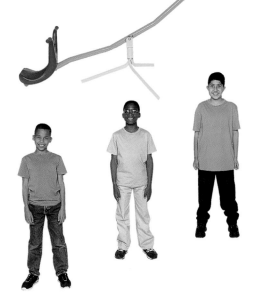

1 Two of you sit on the seesaw, one at each end. Try to achieve a level balance, with your feet off the ground.

In focus

WORK, LOAD, AND DISTANCE

Levers, such as seesaws, make work easier by reducing the force needed to move a load—by spreading it out over a greater distance. Mathematically, the work done equals the force times the distance. The amount of work needed to move a load is always the same, if the effect of friction is not taken into account. What can change is the distance. A small force can do the same work as a large force—and so move as heavy a load—if it works over a greater distance. In other words, the force must be farther from the fulcrum or pivot—or the load closer to it. With a seesaw, one person can balance two people or even lift them, simply by moving farther away from the pivot.

What is happening?

If two people sit on each end of a seesaw, equally far from the pivot in the center, they must be of equal weight to balance. However, if one moves nearer the center, the effect of his weight—his leverage—is reduced. So a person of equal weight at the far end lifts him high in the air, making it impossible to balance. Indeed, as the final step shows, one person can balance two other people of equal weight, if he is far enough from the pivot to give maximum leverage even if they are close to it.

2 Move one seat nearer the center, or let one person sit nearer the center. Now try to balance; you will find it difficult.

With the seat still in the same place as in Step 2, get two people to sit on that end. See if you can get the seesaw to balance now. The weight of two people on one end may now seem to push this end down too much. If so, move the seat on the other end farther out, or simply lean backward. Try different combinations of people on each end, and different combinations of seat positions. Aim to achieve a level balance each time.

WHEELS AND AXLES

Wheels are very rarely used by themselves. Instead, they are mounted on a shaft called an axle, which is attached to the middle, or hub, of the wheel. Sometimes the axle is fixed to the wheel and moves around with it; sometimes the axle goes through a hole in the wheel and the wheel turns around it.

The most obvious use of wheels and axles is on cars and trains, but there are many less obvious uses. Round door knobs are wheels and axles. So are faucets, the control knobs on a stereo system, and CDs when they are playing. In fact, almost every time something turns in a circle, there is likely to be a wheel and axle.

Wooden spoked wheels like the ones on this horse cart have been used all over the world for thousands of years.

In focus

SPOKED WHEELS

The first wheels were discs shaped from solid wood or three planks lashed together. Around 4,000 years ago, wheelbuilders as far apart as Scandinavia, China, and Asia Minor realized they could make light, strong wheels with spokes—bars that radiate from the wheel's hub, or center, to support the rim. For almost 4,000 years, these spokes were made of wood, but in 1808 George Cayley invented very light, wire-spoked wheels, which James Starley developed for bicycles in 1870.

A wheel and axle has many benefits. First, it makes it easy to achieve a smooth, continuous movement. Second, it enables someone to move something a long way while barely moving from the spot—imagine if all the grooves on an old long-playing record were stretched out in a long line.

Third, a wheel and axle is a lever—that is, a device that increases effective effort (see page 6). Because the rim is some way from the hub, a force applied at the rim to turn the

(see page 6)

Did you know?

The gigantic Millennium Wheel was erected in London in the year 2000 to celebrate the millennium.

THE WORLD'S BIGGEST WHEEL

The biggest wheels are Ferris wheels—huge vertical wheels invented by American engineer George Ferris to carry people high in the air for the thrill of it. The world's biggest is the 500-ft. (150-m) tall Millennium Wheel, or London Eye, in London. It carries people around in 32 capsules to give them a spectacular view of the city. There are plans to build an even bigger wheel in France.

axle is multiplied. The bigger the wheel is, the farther the rim is from the hub, and so the more the force is multiplied.

This lever effect is so useful that wheels and axles may first have been used simply to lift weights, for instance, to wind up buckets from wells. In these winding devices, or windlasses, there is an axle but no wheel. Instead, the axle is turned by a handle or crank.

GOING AROUND

You will need

- ✓ A couple of heavy books
- ✓ Some round (not hexagonal) pencils
- ✓ Small marbles of equal size
- ✓ Sugar cubes
- ✓ A flexible ruler (available at arts and crafts stores)

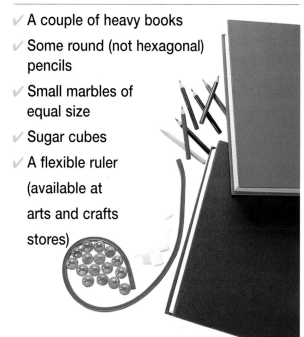

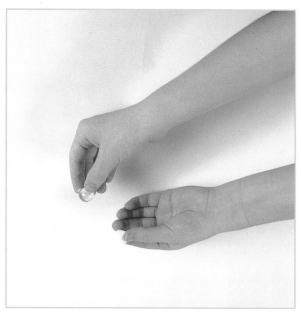

1 See how much farther a round object moves for the same effort by bowling a marble and sugar cube across a table.

In the real world

This cutaway view of a gearbox shows steel balls in a ball bearing around a drive shaft.

BALL BEARINGS

Where a part in a machine slides or rolls past another, it is usually supported by what is called a bearing. The bearing reduces rubbing that would sap power and also wear out the machine. A wheel needs a bearing at the place where it is mounted on an axle. On most early wheels, the bearing was just a collar of wood or leather lubricated with animal fat. Nowadays, most wheels are joined to axles by rolling bearings. Rolling bearings are made from hardened steel balls, rollers (cylinders), or cones that run in a circular groove around the axle.

2 Bend a flexible ruler to make a complete circle, then place about twelve identical-sized marbles inside the circle.

3 Carefully place two heavy books on top of the loop of marbles, then try sliding the books gently around the table.

What is happening?

With the marbles in a loop, you created a simple ball bearing, a device used in a huge range of machines to make it easier for things to move together. But, although you can swivel the books freely, you cannot move them far before they come off the bearings. Moving the books on the pencils shows how people made the first steps toward moving heavy things over a distance on wheeled transport, by placing sleds on rollers. The huge stones that were used to build monuments in the ancient world were probably moved this way.

Now try moving the books by placing them on round pencils instead. The books soon run off your pencil rollers, but, as each pencil comes out from behind the books, take it around to the front, so that the books slide on to it. In this way, you can move the books as far as you like.

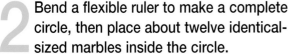

PULLEYS AND CRANES

The hook that carries the load on this crane is attached to a pulley. This reduces by half the effort required to lift it.

For hoisting things straight up, the best simple machine is a pulley. This can be as simple as a rope flung over a bar. Pulling down on one end of the rope lifts a load tied to the other end of the rope. The task is made easier if the rope is run over a grooved wheel called a sheave, rather than a bar.

A single pulley does not cut the load; it works because pulling down is easier than lifting. A single pulley also means you can lift things high above your head, such as when hoisting a flag up a flagpole.

If it is free to move, however, a single pulley may cut the load as well. One end of the rope is fixed to a beam while the pulley

In the real world

Cranes are machines that lift heavy objects with a pulley. In cranes called derricks, the pulley is attached to a long beam called a jib, or boom, and the pulley rope is usually wound in by a powerful motor. The biggest derricks are often mounted on floating barges to lift bridgework and salvage wrecks. The *Musashi* is a floating derrick crane built in Japan in 1974 that can lift over 3,000 tons.

Did you know?

Cable cars whisk people swiftly and easily to the top of mountains. They hang from a wheel running on one cable, while they are hauled up by a pulley system driven by motors at the top or bottom. The world's highest is near the Venezuelan city of Mérida. It is 7.6 miles (12 km) long and climbs almost to the top of Pico Espejo (Mirror Peak) at 15,600 feet (4,750 m).

Cable cars use motorized pulleys to hoist people up mountains.

is attached directly to the load. Then, as the loose end of the rope is pulled up, the pulley moves with the load. This divides the load between the two halves of the rope, and so halves the effort needed to lift it—but the rope must be pulled twice as far.

Another way to cut the load is to combine pulleys—looping the rope first around one pulley, then others. This works by dividing the load between the strands of rope —the more strands there are, the more the load is cut. The load moves a shorter distance for each pull on the rope, but the lifting force is multiplied. Double, or even triple, pulleys are put into a system called a block and tackle. Here the pulleys are housed together inside a case called the block. The tackle is the rope.

SIMPLE PULLEYS

You will need

✓ A spring balance
✓ A long pole
✓ Length of rope
✓ A large bucket
✓ Water

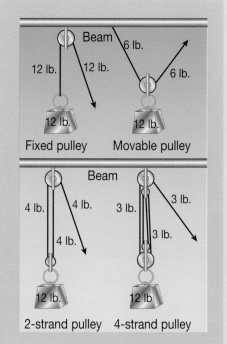

1 Tie a rope to the balance. Hang a bucket of water from the balance hook and lift it by the rope. Check the weight.

In focus

HOW PULLEYS CUT THE LOAD

As with levers, pulley wheels cut a load by spreading it over a greater distance. A single pulley wheel can reduce the load if the rope is fixed at one end and the load hangs directly from the pulley so that the pulley moves with the load. Since both halves of the rope support the load equally, the load is split between them, so the force needed to pull the rope is halved. This system is said to give a mechanical advantage, or MA, of 2. But halving the load means halving the distance it moves, so for every two feet the rope is pulled the load is only lifted one foot. When there is more than one wheel, the MA equals the number of strands of rope. But each increase in the MA means a corresponding increase in the distance the rope must be pulled.

What is happening?

Looping the rope over the bar creates a simple pulley. Lifting the bucket with the pulley is much easier than lifting it directly in the air. Yet, however you measure the weight, the load of the bucket is always the same. So this kind of pulley does not reduce the load. It simply makes lifting easier by allowing you to pull it from a better direction. To actually reduce the load, you need a movable pulley wheel (see "In focus") or a system of interlinked pulley wheels.

2 Now find a fixed railing or set up a bar between two chairs to act as a pulley. Loop the rope over the bar.

Make sure your pulley is fixed firmly in place. Now try pulling the rope down to lift the bucket up. You should find this takes much less effort than lifting it directly, as in Step 1. Try pulling the rope at different angles—horizontally, at 45°, and straight down. Which one needs the least effort? Once you have decided, pull the rope at that angle and look at the weight indicated on the balance. Has it changed? Does it change if you tie the bucket to the other end of the rope and pull directly on the balance hook?

TURNING FORCES

Every force acts in a specific direction. A dart flies in the direction you throw it, gravity makes things fall, and so on. Indeed, all forces act in a straight line. Yet many things turn, from car wheels to entire galaxies. Straight line forces can make things turn when they create what are called turning effects.

Turning effects occur when a force is applied in one place to an object that is fixed in another place, called the fulcrum, or pivot point. The effect is that the force turns the object around the fulcrum. When a person opens a door, the person is the force, the door hinges are the fulcrum, and

When a train crosses the unsupported center sections of Scotland's Forth bridge, its weight exerts a turning force on the bridge, trying to pivot it from the towers.

Did you know?

When bones are broken, it is usually because they are subjected to turning effects, measured in torque. The torque needed to break each bone varies. Breaking the ulna, one of the lower arm bones, takes just 4.5 pound-feet (20 newtons/m). Breaking a thighbone takes 31.5 lb.-ft. (140 newtons/m).

the door swings open in a turning effect.

The turning effect of a force depends on the size of the force and how far away from the fulcrum the force is applied. The farther away the force, the greater the turning effect. The size of a turning force is called a moment.

Sometimes, a turning effect is created not by a single force but by two opposite forces. A bicycle rider turns the handlebars, for instance, by pulling on one side

A bicycle's pedals are turned by the force of each foot pushing alternately on opposing levers, or cranks.

BIKE PEDALS

When bicycle pedals are pushed around, the pedals swing in opposite directions, so it looks as if the pedal wheel is being turned by a couple. This is not strictly true, because the lower foot does not pull the pedal up; it simply rests, letting the other do the work. In fact, the pedals are turned by alternating single force turning effects. Each pedal is a kind of lever called a crank.

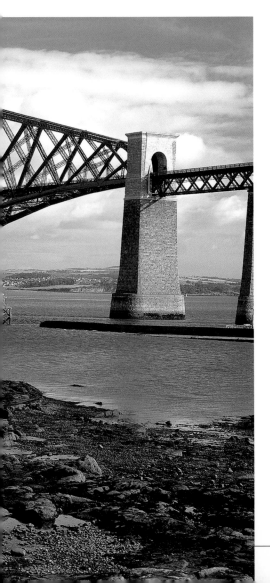

and pushing on the other. Pairs of opposite forces like this are called couples. Car steering wheels, screwdrivers, and faucets are all couples.

The force creating a turning effect is called torque. Torque depends on the force and its distance from the pivot, so is measured in pound-feet (or newtons per meter). These are not to be confused with foot-pounds and newton-meters, which are measures of energy.

CANTILEVERS

You will need

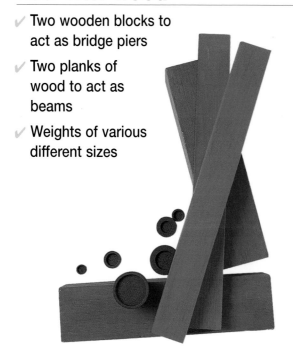

- Two wooden blocks to act as bridge piers
- Two planks of wood to act as beams
- Weights of various different sizes

1 Rest a beam over the pier (block) so most of it projects over one side. Place weights on the short side to balance it.

CANTILEVER BRIDGES

Cantilever bridges are built by projecting out two rigid beams from towers on opposite sides of a river to meet each other in the middle. The towers support the weight of the beams. Wooden cantilever bridges built from logs weighted down with stones were built thousands of years ago in ancient China. But, in recent years, big cantilever bridges have been built from steel to carry heavy loads across water. Often a tower adds extra support in the middle. Famous cantilever bridges include the Forth rail bridge in Scotland and the Quebec Bridge in Canada.

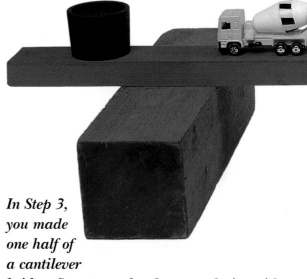

In Step 3, you made one half of a cantilever bridge. Set up another beam and pier with weights in the same way, but with this beam projecting in the opposite direction. Match up the constructions to create a cantilever bridge.

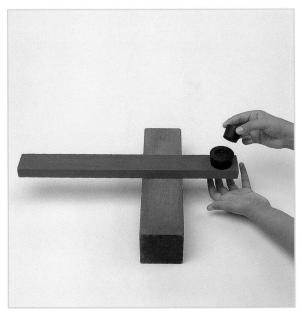

2 Slide the beam over toward the short side. You should find you need less weight to make it balance.

3 Place a small weight (or model trucks) on the projecting beam. Add weights on the short end to balance it.

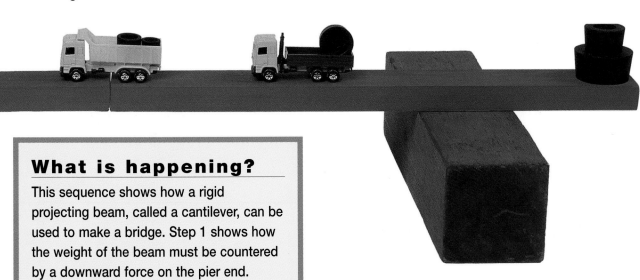

What is happening?

This sequence shows how a rigid projecting beam, called a cantilever, can be used to make a bridge. Step 1 shows how the weight of the beam must be countered by a downward force on the pier end. Step 2 shows how the force needed can be lessened. Step 3 shows how engineers must allow for the weight of traffic on the bridge. Step 4 shows the completed bridge.

GEARS

Nearly every machine that has spinning parts has gears. Some gears make it easier to cycle uphill, or make it easier for a car to pull away from standstill. Gears in an old-fashioned clock ensure that a single motor can drive the minute and hour hands at different rates.

Gears are basically pairs of wheels that turn together, making one axle or shaft turn another. Typically, the edges of the wheels are serrated with chunky teeth. Toothed gear wheels are called cogs. The teeth interlock, or "mesh," so that one cog pushes the other around with minimum slippage.

Gears have a number of different purposes. Some are designed to enable one rotating shaft to turn another in the opposite direction. Some are

Did you know?

Bicycle gears enable riders to keep pedaling at the most efficient rate, or "cadence," for the muscles. For most riders, a cadence of about 60 to 90 turns of the pedals a minute uses muscle power very efficiently. Racing cyclists work well at 75 to 120 turns a minute. Mountain bikers, on the other hand, may often have to work at rates of less than 50 a minute on steep climbs.

In focus

GEAR RATIOS

When the gears in a pair are of different sizes, one turns faster than the other—just how much faster depends on the gear ratio. The gear ratio is the number of times one gear turns for each turn of the other gear. When one gear turns four times for each turn of the other, the gear ratio is 4:1. Most gears have interlocking teeth, and a simple way of assessing gear ratio is to compare the number of teeth on each gear wheel. If there are 48 teeth on one gear and 12 on the other, the ratio is 4:1.

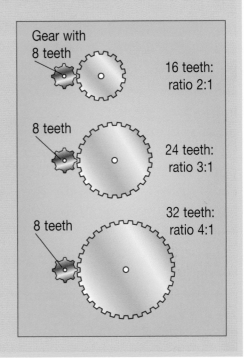

Gear with 8 teeth — 16 teeth: ratio 2:1

8 teeth — 24 teeth: ratio 3:1

8 teeth — 32 teeth: ratio 4:1

designed to allow a shaft at one angle to drive another shaft at a different angle. But most are designed to boost or reduce speed or turning force.

Gears can change speed if the two cogs are of different sizes. When a big cog turns with a little cog, the little cog will turn much faster than the big cog. This is because the rim of the big cog is much longer. So, as the two turn together, the big cog only turns a little way around while the little cog turns all the way around.

It doesn't matter which of the two cogs is driving and which is being driven; when the cogs in a pair are different sizes, the

bigger cog always turns slower than a little cog. The bigger cog also always turns with more force than the little one. This is because the distance from the rim to the center is greater with the big wheel, and so the leverage with which it is turned is much greater.

So when you use a big cog to drive a small cog, you get an increase in speed and a reduction in force. This is what a cyclist needs, for instance, for cycling fast along the flat. When a small cog drives a big cog, the effect is a reduction in speed and an increase in force. This is what a cyclist needs for climbing a steep hill.

DIFFERENT GEARS

Some gears are pairs of wheels or cogs with interlocking teeth. But gears can take many different forms.

The simplest kind of gear is a spur gear. This is a wheel with teeth cut straight across the rim that mesh with the teeth on another spur gear. The second (driven) gear turns on a shaft parallel to the first (driving) gear, but in reverse.

A third gear wheel, called an idler gear, may be placed in between the two gears to make them both turn the same way. The idler then turns in the opposite direction to the driving gear, and so turns the driven gear the same way.

There are other ways gear teeth can mesh besides the straight cut of spur gears. The teeth may be cut at an angle to make bevel gears, or in a spiral to make helical and worm gears (see "In focus").

Racing cyclists still use the simple and elegant gear shifting system developed by Tullio Campagnolo in the 1930s.

In the real world

BICYCLE GEARS

Bicycle gearing starts with the chain drive, said to have been developed by Leonardo da Vinci in the 15th century. But a chain alone is not enough. To pedal easily uphill, the chain is switched to progressively bigger cogs on the back wheel. This system was invented by Frenchman Paul de Vivie in 1905 and perfected by Italian racer Tullio Campagnolo in 1933.

In fact, gears can be made without using toothed wheels at all. One wheel must just turn another of a different size. The wheels do not even need to touch. They can instead be linked by a belt or chain looped around both wheels. A bicycle chain links the big pedal wheel with a smaller wheel on the back wheel. Industrial turning machines are often driven by strong rubber belts, rotated by wheels at either end.

KINDS OF GEARS

The shafts that gears turn on can be at almost any angle to each other, but different angles require different gears. Spur gears are simple gear wheels that interlock with their shafts parallel. Bevel gears are cone shaped so that when the teeth mesh, the shafts are at right angles. Helical gears have a spiral tooth pattern, allowing the shafts to be at an angle to each other. This is very good for transmitting heavy loads. Worm gears have a large gear wheel that meshes with a spiral of teeth and allows one shaft to lie across the other. Rack-and-pinions have a small straight gear (the pinion) that rolls to and fro along a row of teeth (the rack). Car steering gears works like this. In planetary gears, a number of straight gears run around a central gear inside a ring with gear teeth on the inside. This arrangement can give different gear ratios from a single input shaft and so is often used in automatic gearboxes.

Spur gear

Bevel gear

Helical gear

Worm gear

Rack-and-pinion

Planetary gears

Experiments in Science

Science is about knowledge: it is concerned with knowing and trying to understand the world around us. The word comes from the Latin word, *scire*, to know.

In the early 17th century, the great English thinker Francis Bacon suggested that the best way to learn about the world was not simply to think about it, but to go out and look for yourself—to make observations and try things out. Ever since then, scientists have tried to approach their work with a mixture of observation and experiment. Scientists insist that an idea or theory must be tested by observation and experiment before it is widely accepted.

All the experiments in this book have been tried before, and the theories behind them are widely accepted. But that is no reason why you should accept them. Once you have done all the experiments in this book, you will know the ideas are true not because we have told you so, but because you have seen for yourself.

All too often in science there is an external factor interfering with the result which the scientist just has not thought of. Sometimes this can make the experiment seem to work when it has not, as well as making it fail. One scientist conducted lots of demonstrations to show that a clever horse called Hans could count things and tap out the answer with his hoof. The horse was indeed clever, but later it was found that rather than counting, he was getting clues from tiny unconscious movements of the scientist's eyebrows.

This is why it is very important when conducting experiments to be as rigorous as you possibly can. The more casual you are, the more "eyebrow factors" you will let in. There will always be some things that you cannot control. But the more precise you are, the less these are likely to affect the outcome.

What went wrong?

However careful you are, your experiments may not work. If so, you should try to find out where you went wrong. Then repeat the experiment until you are absolutely sure you are doing everything right. Scientists learn as much, if not more, from experiments that go wrong as those that succeed. In 1929, Alexander Fleming discovered the first antibiotic drug, penicillin, when he noticed that a bacteria culture he was growing for an experiment had gone moldy—and that the mold seemed to kill the bacteria. A poor scientist would probably have thrown the moldy culture away. A good scientist is one who looks for alternative explanations for unexpected results.

Glossary

cantilever: A rigid beam or structure fixed only at one end. To stop the unsupported end dropping, there must be a downward force on the fixed end.

crank: A rod with two right angle bends in opposite directions connected to a wheel or axle. It changes a turning motion into a to-and-fro motion.

efficiency: In most machines, friction between moving parts takes up a lot of energy. Efficiency is that percentage of the work put into a machine that is left to move the load.

effort: The force applied to a machine to move the load.

fulcrum: The point at which a lever pivots.

inclined plane: A slope that makes it easier to lift something over a distance.

load: The force resisting movement in a machine.

Mechanical Advantage (MA): A measure of how much

easier a machine makes a task. MA is the force coming out of the machine divided by the force put in.

moment: A measure of how strongly something is being turned. It is worked out by multiplying the turning force by its distance from the pivot.

pinion: A small gear driving or driven by a large gear.

pivot: The fixed point around which something turns.

screw: One of the five simple machines—basically a shaft with a spiral groove, or thread. It works as an inclined plane. The thread makes the screw move forward with much more force than is used to turn it.

torque: The force with which an object turns. It is usually expressed as the average force for each unit of distance from the pivot.

turning effect: How a force acting in a straight line at one place on an object turns

it if the object is held at another place, called the pivot.

Velocity Ratio (VR): Machines often gain power by spreading out the effort over a greater distance than the load moves. VR is the distance moved by the effort divided by the distance moved by the load.

wedge: A triangular block inserted into a gap to force the sides apart. It works partly by converting a direct force such as a hammer blow into a sideways force in the gap, and partly as a pair of inclined planes, boosting the effect of the force.

windlass: A rope wound around a rod turned by a long handle—like the handle for winding a bucket from a well. The handle is a crank, and together with the rod forms a wheel and axle.

work: Work is a measure of the amount of effort used in moving something. It is worked out by multiplying the force used by the distance the object moves.

Index